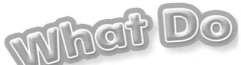

Lisa Trumbauer

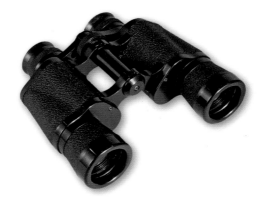

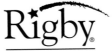

Rigby
A Harcourt Achieve Imprint

www.Rigby.com
1-800-531-5015

I see a tree.

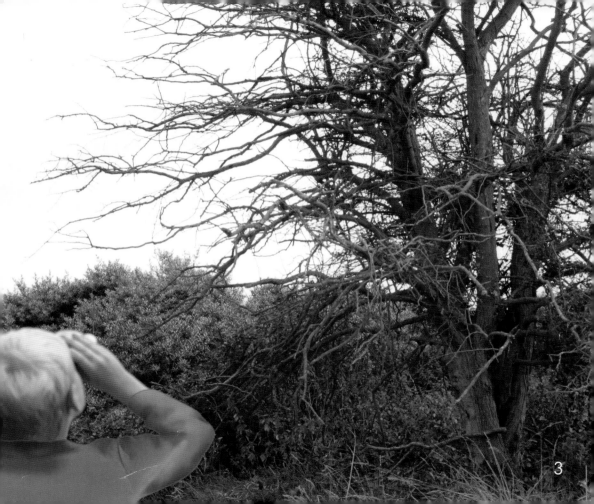

I see a nest.

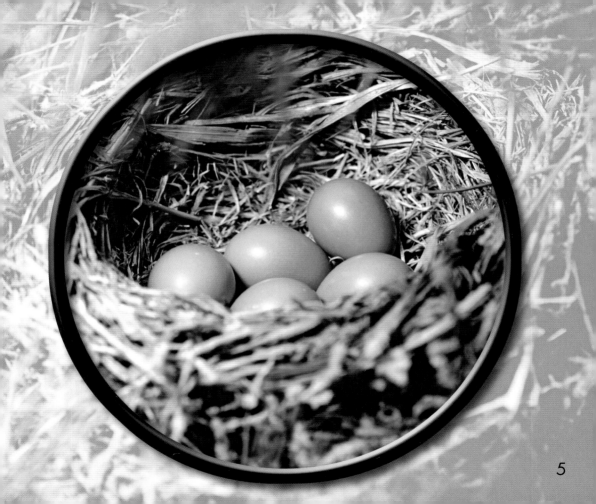

I see a feather.

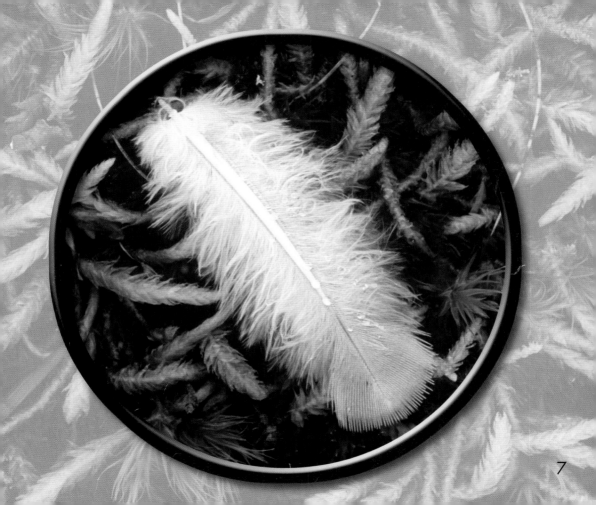

I see a shell.

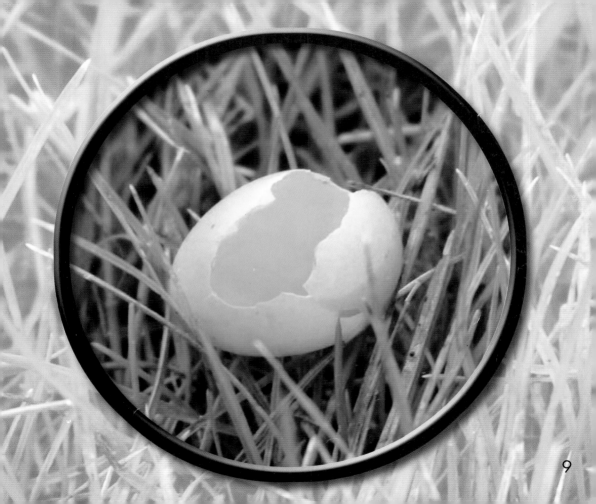

I see a baby.

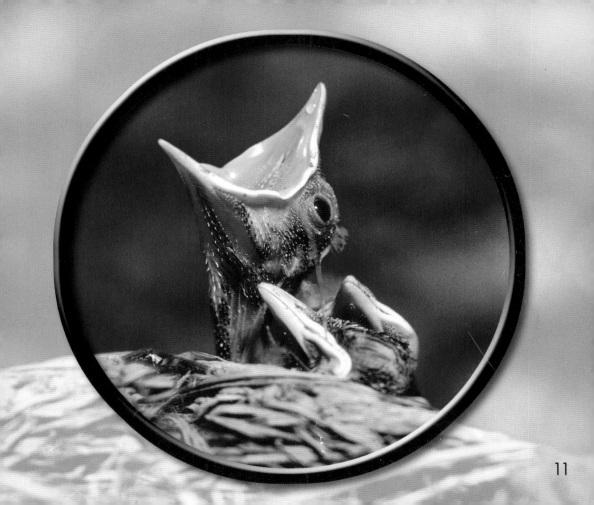

I see a bird.

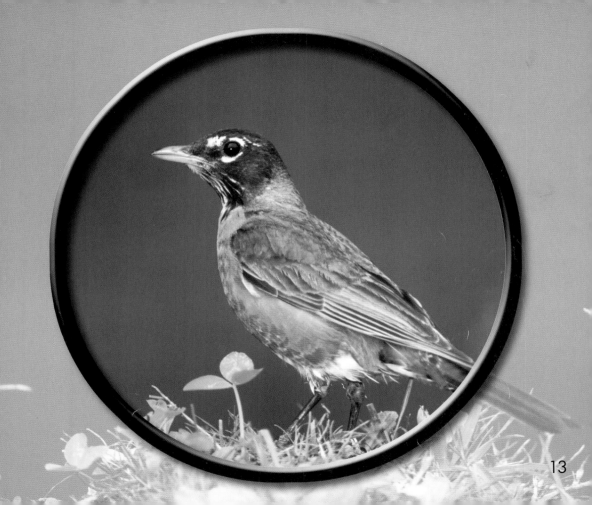

I see a worm.

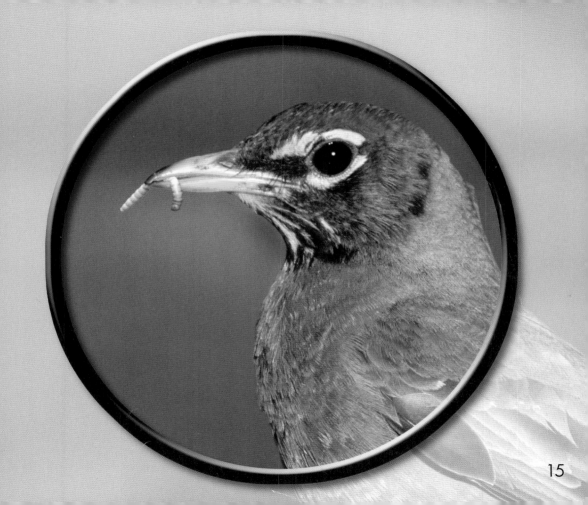

I see a family!

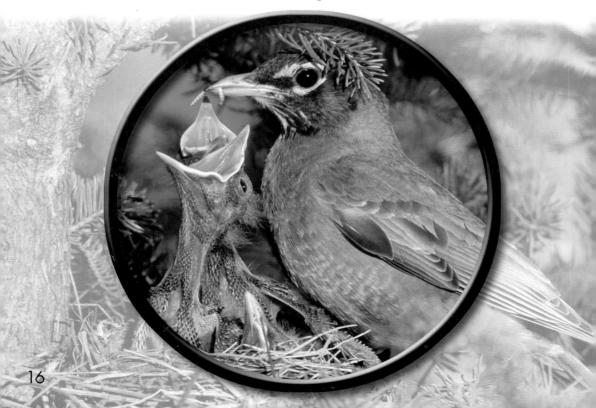